The Badass Single Mom's Survival Guide

H.M. Hudson

DEDICATION

For Lucas, who inspires me every day to be as badass a mom as I can be.

CONTENTS

MY STORY

We live in the age of experts. The age of real ones and lots of self-appointed ones, most with the good intentions to help us live better, more fulfilling lives. Walk into the "Personal Growth" section of any bookstore and if you're not knocked over by the number of titles screaming to help you, you should be. It would probably take a few light years to read through them all.

So, what is this little book about then?

Well, first, it's little. Second, I'm not an expert, but just another single parent who has been bushwhacking my way through the trials and tribulations of this solo voyage for quite a few years now. This little book is a collection of experiences, tips, and ideas on how to steer the course. If it helps you, fantastic, I'm thrilled and I will have accomplished my mission. If not, don't hesitate to write me and ask for your money back. I'll send it and I won't be offended – I promise.

A little about me and how I got here: essentially, I'm just a Midwestern girl, a product of the cornfields and small town life of that vast state of Ohio that most people's experience of is usually along the lines of "Oh yeah, I drove through there once."

I was married to a wonderful man for eight years who I had met and fallen in love with when we were both actors in New York in our early 30s. Shortly after getting married, we upped stakes and moved from New York to London, England, because he had family there and we were ready for a new adventure. Being a child of older parents, they had both passed on when I was in my 20s, the idea of starting a family abroad and far from home didn't phase me a bit. In fact, I had grown up crisscrossing the globe with my own family, due to my father's work, so I was excited by the new challenge and the chance to give my as yet unborn children dual citizenship so they might truly become citizens of the world.

Things didn't go quite according to plan. Fast-forward six years, and we have a five-year-old little boy (The Boy) my husband, "Tim," is undergoing a full-on mid-life meltdown, peppered with the usual array of vices. Needless to say, our marriage crashed and burned, bankruptcy ensued, husband fled to Spain, a good choice of a place for finishing out a mid-life crisis and avoiding responsibility.

The Boy and I took refuge in the warm, embracing folds of my hometown back in Ohio, also affectionately known as the Womb with a View. I never in a million years thought I'd find myself living there again, but was I ever grateful to be able to land in such a place.

Tim eventually recovered enough to visit once in a blue moon before moving back to England and remarrying. So I have mostly, been sole parenting my amazingly wonderful boy, with the moral support of my eldest brother and his wife as well as a bevy of new and old friends.

My goal has always been to create a lifestyle that supports both the Boy and I. Meaning that I am around as much as possible for him and I don't lose my mind trying to make a 9 to 5 job work, which I'm not very good at! So I cobble together freelance work as a writer. I am no cushy, trust fund baby. In fact, I have worked an array of jobs to piece things together when I've been between freelance gigs. This has even included stints waiting tables at The Olive Garden (now there are some stories, trust me).

The most important thing to me is that I am truly location independent. I am a traveler at heart and I have always been determined there was no way simply being a single parent was going to keep the Boy and I from having these experiences. My parents had given me the opportunity to live abroad for various stints growing up, so I wanted to find some way to do the same for him, even if it didn't include an ex-pat relocation package.

And traveling we did. Over the last several years, we spent extended stints of time in the UK, Germany, Italy, and France. We travel less now than we did a few years ago, mainly because the Boy is in high school and is uber-serious about playing soccer.

So, if you are single, have embraced the concept of quality of life and independence, then take these 21 tips as a bit of hard earned wisdom gleaned along my own journey. Take what works, throw away what doesn't. You got this.

"It takes a village to raise a child."
— African proverb

#1 – BUILD YOUR COMMUNITY

So basic as to almost go without saying, but none of us can do everything by ourselves. We need friends, family, and community. You might have any of these in varying degrees, depending on your circumstances, but forget any kind of superhero complex you might have, and reach out to those who might be able to help you, whether its having a shoulder to cry on, bitch and moan to, or help with childcare, it all helps.

By now, everyone has heard the overused phrases find your tribe or your vibe attracts your tribe. There's a reason sayings catch on and become well worn phrases in our popular lexicon. But I prefer to use the word community instead. It seems less of an assimilated word and more authentic to our western culture. After all, if I recall, we colonized a lot of Native American tribes when building this new country. It seems a bit two-faced to now go and start calling ourselves "tribes."

To get to the important point, it's really about being your authentic self and how you attract those you seek out by virtue of sharing similar interests and outlooks on life. This can be easier said than done when you are juggling your kids' lives, your work, keeping your household running, and all that goes into being a single mom, right? And the truth is, the people who are going to be your friends when you have young kids, especially, are the parents of your kids' friends. That's just how it works. The

4

path of least resistance plays out on a day-to-day level. As it should, because in fact, these are the people who are, by nature, members of your community. You will have the most in common with another mom raising a similar age kid, who has similar interests to your own.

Here are some ways you can build a community of support for you and your kids:

- Collect responsible babysitters and create a spreadsheet with their contact details – 13 to 16-year-olds make the world's best babysitters, and good boy babysitters are like gold dust. At this age, girls and boys alike are eager to make their own money, prove their responsibility, and are not yet too caught up in a high school social life or heavy duty academic work (some, but not all!).

- Create a babysitting network with other single parent friends, offering to supervise someone else's kids for an evening on a rotating schedule with all people offering same.

- Use social networking wisely. Join or create a Facebook page for local single parents. You can swap ideas, services, potluck dinners, meet ups, recommendations on providers, the list is endless and can provide connections if you don't have built in ones through family or your kids' friends.

- Join a church or community group. The latter especially, even if you don't consider yourself religious or the church-going type. Churches often have mother groups and provide daycare. Then you're meeting people who are in the same phase of life as you and your kids get to have fun and make friends in the process too.

- Join Mommy and Me classes or any other sport or activity, like swimming lessons for little ones, which involve you and your kids. There are no better people to meet than other moms with kids -- they are your community!

"To weep is to make less the depth of grief."
— William Shakespeare

#2 – GRIEVE AND MOVE ON

Even if ending the marriage or partnership was your choice, there is still grief for the loss of the marriage itself, for what might/should have been, for the fact that your children won't be growing up with two parents in a loving relationship with each other. It's hard and it takes a lot of time. It's also not as if there is any set amount of time that is acceptable or normal to grieve nor does it happen in a linear way.

I have learned, from not only going through a divorce myself, but also a miscarriage and losing both my parents at a fairly young age, that grief is an odd beast. It is always with you and it rears its head just when you think you have slayed the thing. But better to roll with it, meet it head on, and after a few rounds of that, you will get stronger every time and more ready to make space in your life for new things, people, and relationships. In the meantime, keep these points in mind in the early days of the grief process:

- Mood swings are normal and just give yourself permission to feel downright crappy about things.
- Stay connected to others. Even if you feel silly contacting that friend from high school on Facebook – it's good to reach out whenever and wherever possible.
- While you don't want to endlessly analyze what happened, it's also important to understand old patterns before embarking on new relationships,

especially as the fall-out from rebound relationships can have an adverse knock-on effect on your kids. So finding a counselor or therapist to talk to can be a really wise investment in your mental and emotional health.

- Finally, quit reminding yourself you're single every day. Better to be single and healthy than in a bad relationship!

"Motivation is what gets you started. Habit is what keeps you going."
– Jim Ryan

#3 – Get Enough Sleep and Stay Healthy

This goes back to the idea of putting on your oxygen mask before you put it on your kid – if you don't take care of yourself, you can't take care of anybody else! While regular exercise is just not always possible (who has that kind of time?) there are some great resources out there for making the most of the time you do have to keep fit and healthy. Marks Daily Apple has loads of tips on getting exercise in some unusual ways at home – simply working with what you have and also great, nutritious recipes.

But if you're not always feeling so Amazonian as some of those cross-fitters and Paleo diet zealots can sometimes make you feel, check out Go Kaleo for some more moderate and down-to-earth health and fitness advice. Amber Rogers has learned things the hard way and has a lot of great wisdom to share.

Also, we have been led to believe by mainstream media that if we don't get at least 30 minutes of cardio a day, we are failing ourselves and putting our future health at risk. All this generally leads to is a nagging sense of guilt that we can never live up the holy grail of health and exercise. And this, dear reader, is just nonsense. By and large, if you are mindful of what you put in your mouth and ingest as food, and keep moving throughout the day, rather than being mostly sedentary, you are more than half way there. Do not fall victim to the mindset that exercise can cure everything when nutrition is neglected. Eat more real food, less processed food and carbohydrates and you will make substantial changes not only to your health, but your waistline, more so than hours spent on any elliptical machine.

Even though it's been years since Dr. Kenneth Cooper, the father of the aerobic craze that began in the '70s and '80s delicately recanted his stance on aerobic exercise by saying " If your goal is aerobic fitness, then you should exercise at 65-80% of your predicted maximal heart rate. If, on the other hand, your goal is only to maximize health and longevity benefits, you should exercise below that level—something I never thought I'd say." Our obsession with aerobic exercise lives on in the mainstream media. Ignore it. There are viable alternatives that also just so happen to suit the busy lifestyles of most of us.

Again, if you are getting enough sleep and staying healthy, you will be better able to make sure your kids are doing the same. A recent study from Boston College revealed that the United States has the highest number of sleep deprived students in the world, with 73% of 9 and 10-year-olds and 80% of 13 and 14-year-olds identified by their teachers as being adversely affected by lack of sleep. Such chronic sleep deprivation can manifest as hyperactivity, making it yet harder to fall asleep and thus creating a vicious cycle. A major culprit identified by the study was electronic activity in bedrooms. Try limiting all such activity for all family members an hour before bedtime to allow for decompression time. Not to mention, limit any intake of caffeine or sugar before bed.

"It's easier to prevent bad habits than to break them."
— Benjamin Franklin

#4 – Avoid Using Alcohol / Smoking / Food as a Crutch

This is a tough one and I know because I've been there. I lived in England for the first five years of The Boy's life and the UK is unabashedly a drinking culture. Kids' birthday parties were always replete with wine for the parents as little Hannah and Orlando bounced in the bouncy castle. Nor was there ever any shame in joking with another mother as you dropped your wee one off for a playdate, "Is it wine o'clock yet?" But this starts to wear thin when all of a sudden your child is ten and you realize he's been watching you pour the proverbial glass of evening Merlot for the better part of his life he can remember.

Or your crutch could be food or smoking weed. Whatever it may be, it's become that one thing that you rely on to give you just a little relief at the end of the day. It's hard to challenge yourself on these things and move out of your comfort zone. But when you stop to think about the fact that we are constantly modeling behaviors for our kids, we have to ask ourselves tough questions that can lead us to realize that maybe some of these behaviors are not so great and even potentially harmful.

Last year I wrote about giving up wine for 30 days on Medium with an essay Why I'm Giving Up Alcohol for 30 Days: Confessions of a Red Wine Lover. It was a wonderful and liberating exercise for me and since then

I've vastly reduced my wine consumption from being an every day occurrence, to limiting it to weekends or special social occasions. Both my sleep and productivity have improved and it has enabled me to better cope with some of the slings and arrows of parenting The Boy who is now a teenager.

There are also signs that sobriety is gaining a sort of cultural cache. In a recent article on www.wanderlust.com, It's Hip to Be Sober, the author explored alternatives to booze culture that are cropping up in cities across America, though notably mostly on the west and east coasts. Wellness communities like Shine and Daybreaker offer alcohol-free raves, dance parties, gatherings, and concerts, which are definitely a different and refreshing take on emerging pop culture offerings.

Of course, it goes without saying, if you really feel like reaching for that drink, joint, or chocolate Ho-Ho has become something that is not just a crutch, but you can't imagine living without, it might be time to face those demons head on and reach out for help to kick the crutch out of the park. Recovery.org is a good starting place for looking at addiction recovery options. Stickk.com is a website that helps you set your goals and achieve them through what they call a commitment contract where you put your own money on the line that you will lose if you don't achieve your goals. Based on the idea of the Ulysses Pact, it forces you to be accountable to yourself. The website Diet Bet works similarly for those trying to lose weight.

Ultimately, the point is to make sure that your crutches aren't controlling you. There is nothing wrong with blowing off steam or rewarding yourself at the end of a long day or celebrating a special occasion. And only you can know where that line is for yourself when you cross it and it becomes something bigger that needs to be dealt with. Benjamin Franklin's words could not have been truer when he said, "It's easier to prevent bad habits, then to break them."

"Housework, if you do it right, will kill you."
— Erma Bombeck

#5 – STICK TO A SCHEDULE

I am actually the worst person to advise sticking to a schedule as I find it hard to do myself, if it is not already imposed by school and working hours. Nevertheless, I find that having a rough plan, even if we end up veering off of it, is a great place to start. I am a huge fan of To Do lists because they help organize my thinking, prioritize, and it just feels so good to be able to cross things off the list, even if it's just a trip to the dry cleaners.

Schedules give rhythms to your day and can help you feel in control of things, even when on the inside you might feel just slightly out of control. Not to mention that kids like to know what things are happening when, even if they are young enough that clock-time is irrelevant to their daily existence. So trying to have dinner, homework, bath-time, bedtime, whatever elements of your day that are staples, at fairly regular times, will help everyone in your household feel more grounded and at ease. And when you know you can finally sit down and pour that glass of wine or have that Bengal Spice tea after 9 o'clock, trust me, it makes getting through those last few hours of the day that much easier. Oh, and just forget the housework, other than the Erma Bombeck basics: if the item doesn't multiply, smell, catch fire, or block the refrigerator door, let it be. No one else cares. Why should you?

"Nothing is softer or more flexible than water, yet nothing can resist it."
— Lao Tzu

#6 – BE FLEXIBLE

Having extolled the virtues of structure and schedule, your survival as a single parent also depends on staying flexible. Being rigid and trying to stick to your schedule when the unexpected arises will only create more strife for you and your kids. Anyone who is a parent is already familiar with the reality of quick adjustments and turnarounds when your 4-year-old comes up in the unexplained rash or develops the raging fever out of nowhere.

Being a single parent is an ongoing juggle and plate spinning exercise, but I'm referring to flexibility in the bigger picture. There are times when we get caught up in how things have always been with our kids, and fail to recognize when what works in the past doesn't work anymore, usually because our kids have outgrown a parenting approach that was right for that age.

I've been guilty of this many times myself. It's easy to lose sight of the changes your child is going through when you see her day in and day out and it takes stepping back sometimes and accepting that she might have reached a new plateau and that sending her to her room for a time-out at age 12, doesn't quite have the same effect as it did when she was 8 or 9.

Being flexible also means admitting, if at least to yourself, that sometimes you are wrong and make mistakes. We can all make knee jerk decisions based on either past experience or fear that sometimes just don't end up working out. It is really OK to change course and admit to your child, and yourself, that you are human and you are allowed to change your mind and make mistakes. Both in terms of letting him do something he wants to do that at first you said no to. Maybe he wants to climb the big oak tree in your front yard and you've said no three times already because all you can see is an expensive trip to the emergency room looming in front of you. You know the one where you don't meet your deductible and get to pay $500 for the privilege of a sling and an X-ray.

But then you think of all the trees you climbed as a kid and you come to your senses and realize, rightly, that trees are for climbing, among other things, and that what is potentially gained is probably more than what is potentially lost. You want to now say yes, but feel that after saying no for so long you will undermine your authority, and create an avalanche of future doom upon your head if you reverse your original decision. This is simply not true. You are human and allowed to change your mind. You just tell your kid, "You know, I've thought about it some more, and I changed my mind." That's all, 'nuff said! The world has not ended and you will proceed with perhaps even more authority going forward because he will realize that you are reasonable person, capable of considering the options, and sometimes admitting that seeing things his way, is actually the better way. Of course, when he's 16 and wants to drive your car with six of his friends in an ice storm, feel free to lure him to the basement, lock it behind him, and ignore all, pleas for mercy until the weather improves.

"To be a good parent, you need to take care of yourself so that you can have the physical and emotional energy to take care of your family."
— Michelle Obama

#7 – MAKE TIME FOR YOURSELF

There is an abiding principle at work when the flight attendant tells you to put your own mask on first before you help your child. That is, quite obviously, that you can't help anyone else without helping yourself first. You can be the selfless, giving parent 98.8% of the time, but in order for that 98.8% to fly, you have to set aside just a little space for yourself to breathe, to refuel, to be you. Even if it's just an hour in the morning before the kids are up, or at night after they're asleep, Guard this time like it's the Crown Jewels capable of paying off your debt and your kids' college education in one fell swoop.

Because it really can.

Making time for yourself can mean different things to different people. Sometimes putting your feet up with a glass of Pinot is all you can manage, but others it's making time for reading, writing, playing the piano, whatever your creative, intellectual, athletic or just outlet might be. Sure, there are stages in our kids' lives' when they simply need us and depend on us utterly and completely. But really, once they get to the age when they can play on their own without fear of choking on a Lego, and can exercise a degree of reasoning and understanding, there is more to be gained from a parent who models behavior that does not revolve around your kid's every need and fancy.

Children who learn how to self-entertain at an earlier age are more likely to be able to self-regulate as they get older as well. So really it's a win-win situation since there will be times when you, as a parent, need to be able to say, "I am going to be in here doing xy and z for the next 45 minutes, and do not disturb me unless there is an emergency." Research also shows that children who learn how to self-regulate at a young age are able to delay gratification as they get older and I don't need to bang on about the usefulness of that skill in life.

One of the simplest ways to start making time for yourself, even in the tiniest of ways, is to meditate for five minutes soon after you wake up, and right before you go to bed at night. Meditating does not require any knowledge of Sanskrit or chanting, it can be as simple as sitting in a quiet placed either with your eyes closed or looking out your window at nature and observing your breathing, the thoughts that flit through your head, the distant sound of a dog barking. I set the timer on my phone for 5 minutes so it chimes when my time is up and I keep moving with my day. It helps ground me just a little bit more before I face the chaos of the day, or unwind before sleep.

"Be a strong woman so your daughter will have a role model and your son will know what to look for in a woman when he's a man."
— Unknown

#8 – IT'S OK TO DATE (AND IT'S OK NOT TO)

This of course goes hand in hand with making time for yourself, but when you are ready, and you've got that babysitting tree up and running, get out there and on some dates. It seems silly to go over the basics of online dating since by this time it has become woven into the fabric of our lives. However, for the newly single who were married before online dating was really a fixture, it can still all seem a bit strange and frankly, dodgy.

But when my 20-something year old niece routinely meets her boyfriends through online dating sites or apps, you realize we've arrived at a plateau where this has become the expected and pre-dominant means to romantic involvement for all ages.

Having said that, a virtual meat-market is not much better than a real one, though going out to a bar or club to actually meet someone can feel both passé and pointless in the 21st century. The biggest fear about online dating for some people is the oft-stated one of "How do you know anybody is who they say they are?" Guess what: that happens in traditional three-dimensional interactions too!

The point is, you find out some basic details about them, filter them through a few email exchanges, have a phone chat, and trust me, if you are of sound mind and instinct you will be able to know whether it's a) worth it and b) safe to meet them for a coffee at Starbucks.

Sifting through profiles and answering emails can start to seem like a monumental job that quickly loses the newly minted air of sexy frisson when you first join up on a site. I've got news for you: it is a job and it's all in the numbers. You've simply got to spin that roulette wheel enough times, have enough coffee or wine dates, before the balance of statistics tips in your direction. OK, I do have one friend who beat all odds and met her life partner after one Internet date, so fluky things happen. But she's an annoying anomaly and we won't talk about her because her experience is certainly not the norm.

Another point to take in here that is important, do not be too rigid in screening people out based solely on looks or a pre-determined list of what their characteristics must be. The most important thing really is to make sure you feel comfortable meeting and you think you might have enough to talk about with for an hour over a coffee.

How do you determine these things before going on a date? Trade enough emails or messages with them to get a basic sense of who they are and how they comport themselves in meeting someone new through written communication back and forth. You'd be amazed at what you can tell about a person from their ability, or lack thereof to write a simple message. A happy medium is possible between the extremes I've personally experienced of "Fancy a vodka and a joint?" to "Your profile reads good. I look for happy woman to spend the rest of my life with." I don't need to point out the abundance of red flags in each approach and no, I didn't meet either of them.

Believe me, I can safely say I am an expert at this by now. If a guy's first approach to you online is "Hey pretty lady, wanna chat?" you can be reasonably sure that he's not interested in really getting to know the inner you. If casual encounters are what you're after, by all means, charge ahead. They're a dime a dozen. But a more cautious and gradual approach is likely to happen from a guy who is more or less after the same thing as you – at least some companionship and exploring the possibility of more.

Even though most of us would probably rather meet people through work or personal introductions, we might also worry about qualifying for social security while we wait around for that to happen. In these cases, online dating can at least be a poor cousin substitute – better yet, a path to true love -- and can give one's ego a bit a boost (or beware, complete deflation!) in the process.

Or you can always try a trick that a friend's mother swears by as she met her second husband this way: find an attractive man in the supermarket, scope out the wedding ring situation, if none, accidentally swap carts with them until they have to talk to you to retrieve theirs. Whoops! Chatting ensues. My friend's mother's future husband followed her to the parking lot and asked for her number. She demurred to give her number to a 'stranger' but invited him to her synagogue social group that weekend. He came and that was that.

So having encouraged you that it's perfectly OK to start dating and a completely healthy way for you to take care of yourself and move forward with your life, it is also really OK to say, 'Meh…no thanks, my plate is full with kids, work, friends, etc. right now." Don't succumb to some silly social pressure from friends or family that you absolutely have to 'get back out there.' The truth is, dating is also a bit of work, especially the online variety as it can be time consuming, and at times demoralizing, sifting through endless profiles and emails. Believe me, a trip to the dentist can be more appealing at times. And hey, if your dentist happens to be cute, why not? You will know when you're ready and there is no right time frame about when you should be. Listen to your gut.

Finally, if you meet that new someone and you really like him (or her) and it's all going swimmingly, be cautious about introducing them to your kids, no matter how old they are. If your kids are young and you haven't been divorced or separated that long, they can become attached to mommy's new friend quickly -- they can also become jealous. And in the early days of dating someone new, there are just so many unknowns still in your own relationship.

Do your kids a favor, and wait until you know if the relationship has legs and seems like it's going to last a while before introducing them into your life with your kids. Of course, there are never any guarantees in life or relationships as we know, but some caution in this department is probably better than none at all.

*"If you want children to keep their feet on the ground,
put some responsibility on their shoulders."*
– Abigail Van Buren

#9 – TEACH YOUR KIDS HOW TO COOK

As soon as they are reasonably old enough to operate safely in the kitchen, start by involving your kids in helping you prepare meals. First of all, cooking together is fun. And when your kids are doing real things with you that matter and there is a visible outcome in the very near future, or simply the prospect of cake, they love it. The problem of course is often you are tired, rushed, and it's just easier to do it all yourself. Because after all, we're great at doing it all ourselves – other people just get in the way most of the time. But the rewards that you will plumb from putting in some time and patience with teaching your kids to cook, will be gold dust later on for both you and them.

Cooking with your kids is also a great learning experience for them. It goes without saying of course that they are learning a life survival skill, but there is math involved, when it comes to measuring things, halving recipes, and figuring portions. These are also fantastic opportunities for your kids to learn about nutrition and healthy eating, something that is sadly an afterthought in the standard educational setting, other than some pretty multi-colored pictures of the standard USDA food pyramid from time to time.

Finally, and the best part in my opinion, is cooking is creative. It involves experimentation, instinct and creative flair. Check out Jamie Oliver videos on YouTube for some great inspiration on cooking with teenagers especially. He's got some wonderful simple recipes that are good starting places. I also highly recommend "Jamie's 15 Minute Meals" cookbook.

Also, don't be afraid to let your kids handle the real tools, like knives. In America especially, we are extremely overprotective of our children. Ellen Hansen Sandseter, a Norwegian academic at Queen Maud University in Norway, reveals through her research that adopting a more relaxed approach to risk-taking and safety has the effect of keeping children safer as they hone their own judgment as to what they are capable of. If their world is a safely padded room, they will never learn what they are capable of and will always be drawn to what we deem dangerous or forbid them to do. Sandseter maintains "the most important safety protection you can give your child is to let them take risks."

So entrust them with real responsibilities in the kitchen. They will enjoy more, learn more quickly, and you will be paving the road for a self-sufficient young person in your house

"The most remarkable thing about my mother is that for thirty years she served the family nothing but leftovers. The original meal has never been found."
– Calvin Trillin

#10 – Cook in Bulk on the Weekend

Once you've got the kids cooking, the next thing is to cook at least one dish in large enough amounts that can be frozen and thawed for lunches or quick dinners during the next week. While it's great if you can be organized enough to have meals planned and posted on your fridge during the week with cooking assignments attached, that is a level of organization that I personally rarely achieve.

I prefer the method of loosely planning a few dishes we're going to cook for the week, along with a large casserole type dish that lends itself well to freezing, like eggplant parmesan, lasagna, mac and cheese, or mousaka, for example. The loose planning method enables me to have enough of the basic ingredients on hand, but leaves room for what we feel like eating a certain night, and also the unexpected, like running out of time when you're rushing to get to an evening school concert or soccer practice.

Take a dive into the vast compendium of books on frugal, simple living and how to live successfully as a full fledged cheapskate. Warning: the library is huge and be prepared to invest some time here, but the rewards are well worth it for those willing to exercise their creativity and brain in making do with what you have. The wartime phrase "Mend and make do" is something that has been largely lost in our consumer driven culture where virtually everything is disposable and we are always encouraged to throw things out, rather than fix or reuse them.

We must fight the impulse to throw out whenever possible and creatively find uses for items we can't fix. Lifehacker is full of brilliant, funky ideas for making the most of what you've got, plus unusual uses for everyday objects. The Complete Tightwad Gazette is an exhaustive compendium by Amy Dacyczyn that entails six years of her newsletters with suggestions on frugal living for every aspect of life. Even if 13 uses for pickle juice is more information than you need or can use, you're sure to find some useful ideas in here to cut corners and improve your bottom line.

Also, if you don't own a crock pot -- get one! This is another must-own tool for simplifying your life as a single mom. Add all ingredients in the morning and forget about until the end of the day when you have a delectable one-pot meal all ready to serve up for you and your kids. Your local library will probably have many choices of crockpot or one pot meal cookbooks to help you get started with this super easy method of cooking.

"A big part of financial freedom is having your heart and mind free from worry about the what-ifs of life."
— Suze Orman

#11 – AUTOMATE YOUR FINANCIAL LIFE

Automating your financial life as much as humanly possible is critical to your sanity. Who can remember when every bill is due when you're already remembering 17 other things a day, plus meeting everyone's needs, trying to meet you own, and keep income flowing into your household? When I finally woke up and realized I was not losing control by automating my financial life, but gaining it, I have never looked back to the days before these options were available. Unfortunately, not all employers, especially if you happen to be a freelancer, offer the option of Direct Deposit, but this is a wonderful perk if you can take advantage of it.

By scheduling your bill payments online when you know you will have the funds in the bank, and recurring at the same time each month, you will lift a huge burden off your plate and leave time for the more interesting and important aspects of living.

By all means, if you're technical and savvy enough to use any of the financial planning software available on the market, that can be useful to. I just discovered that my online banking portal offers a free money management service once I clicked to be enrolled in it. It includes an easy to reference calendar with all my regular direct debits and deposits, a savings calculator, and a snapshot view of where my money is going each month gathered from my debit card usage, which I use for almost all payments.

This is a useful and sobering tool when you're wondering at the end of the month why that spreadsheet budget you created just does not seem to be comporting with cash in the bank.

"Today, there are three kinds of people: the have's, the have-not's, and the have-not-paid-for-what-they-have's."
— Earl Wilson

#12 – MANAGE YOUR DEBT

Unsecured personal debt can be a de facto way of life for everyone, single or not, but the truth is harsh: one income households are hard to manage. Over the years I have received support payments on an irregular basis, and even when it has come, it's never much. When you find yourself with too much debt to handle there are a number of things you can do and places you can turn to for help. But the first thing you have to do is a) try not to panic, b) stop and admit it's a problem that has to be addressed, c) don't beat yourself up about it, and finally, d) cut up your credit cards – now!

As anyone knows there are countless books and websites out there that you can wade through to begin to sort out the mess. Two of my personal favorite books on getting a handle on and getting out of debt are Your Money or Your Life by Robin & Dominguez and How to Get Out of Debt, Stay Out of Debt, and Live Prosperously by Jerrold Mundis. For a continuously updated and amazing blog that will have you reexamining lifestyle and cultural issues around money, check out Mr. Money Mustache.

The one thing I can't overstate is Don't Panic. Seriously, this is easy to say and hard to do. Being in debt is continually stressful, day in and day out, sort of like a freight train parking itself on your chest, especially at 3am in the morning. Not to minimize the gravity of debt, but you have to do a bit of deft compartmentalization in order to keep going with your life and function as a parent. But what you have to realize is paying the rent or the mortgage is the most important bill of all. Try to put that payment in a separate account if there is a time gap between when you get paid and when that is due, so it doesn't get spent on other necessities.

The next thing is that no credit card company is going to come banging on your door, repossess your furniture and sell your children on the black market. You will have to pay them back, but take a deep breath and figure out a plan and if they have to wait another month or two for their first payments, they will survive. Your survival and the well being of your family is the most important thing.

I had to do this once. I wrote to each creditor that I had and explained my situation, that I was unemployed, actively looking for work and I would start paying them back as soon as I could. I sent them token payments of $10 each. They bitched and moaned, sent threatening letters, and smeared black marks on my credit report. But at the end of the day, it's a credit report and having a good one of those is what helped get you into this mess in the first place! If your goal is true financial freedom for yourself, believe me, your credit rating is the last thing you are going to be worried about when you get there. And surprisingly, when I was able to pay more monthly, I called up their accounts in arrears department and they were helpful in working out a payment plan with me.

The other option, if you prefer not to deal with the credit card companies directly, is to use a debt management and consolidation service like In Charge. They negotiate with your creditors on your behalf; work out one monthly lump sum payment that gets distributed to the creditors through In Charge, to which they add in their fee for their services. This method definitely winds up being more expensive than the do-it-yourself way, but it is effective and it takes the day to day management of things out of your hands. They will also let you know the date you will be debt-free with their money management tools.

Leo Babauta, the writer who maintains the popular blog, Zen Habits, has a wonderful post about how he climbed out of debt slowly and the steps he took to get there. This site is also very useful for ideas on simple living, being mindful of our choices, and stepping back and trying to take in the big picture.

"If you don't like the road you're walking, start paving another one."
— Dolly Parton

#13 – HACK YOUR CAREER

I have a lot of friends who are teachers and it's easy to see why it's a popular career choice for single parents especially. You get to be on roughly the same hours as your kids, often avoiding after-school care costs or the latch key kid situation.

But teaching or working in the educational system is not for everybody. If you find yourself in a situation where your job provides no satisfaction or joy and only stress, it's time to start thinking outside the box for ways to change or increase your income stream. This does not always have to mean a sea change such as going back to night school and completely re-training for another career.

Online courses are abundant, from masters and certificate programs, to a plethora of skills-enhancing courses for money or free, A few examples are edX, The Personal MBA, Kahn Academy (not just for kids' math tutorial videos anymore) and the Small Business Administration. Or simply scroll through the compendium of free TED Talks or free courses at Coursera for a bit of inspiration. I particularly like to find talks that the Boy and I can watch together. So, the sky is really the limit in terms of the number of possibilities and ways to explore increasing your income or re-examining and changing career course.

"My grandmother wanted me to have an education, so she kept me out of school."
— Margaret Mead

#14 – ROLL WITH HOMESCHOOLING

This is a huge topic and boiling down the rationale and essence for homeschooling into a sound bite is not really possible. But suffice it to say, homeschooling is not only the purview of large nuclear families, religious or non-religious. If your kid struggles with the narrow, standardized way that education is delivered in the state or private school system, or any other aspect of school such as bullying, you can still homeschool as a single parent.

It takes some creativity and juggling, but it can indeed be done. The beauty of homeschooling is that whatever work you do, even if you follow an out of the box curriculum, or create your own, can be done whenever you decide it gets done. For two hours every evening, on the weekends, first thing in the morning, you name it. You only need two to three hours of focused time per day, on average and depending on the age of your child, you will achieve the same results that seven hours spent shuffling around in school can achieve. You'll soon realize how much time is wasted in school on things other than learning.

Some people prefer an 'Unschooling' approach to their child's education, which is entirely child-led, without any formal curriculum. Sandra Dodd's site Radical Unschooling is a good place to head if you want to explore that option. For a more formal, classical approach explore The Well Trained Mind and book of the same name. No reading list for homeschooling would be complete without mentioning that any book by John Holt or John Taylor Gatto on the subject is worth reading. Start with How Children Learn by John Holt or Dumbing Us Down, a classic by John Taylor Gatto, an award-winning, retired New York City schoolteacher.

Obviously, homeschooling as a single parent is going to be easier if you have some autonomy and control over your working hours. Also, when kids become a bit more independent and are able to work and occupy themselves with projects on their own for periods of time, this helps as well. But the benefits you can gain from freeing yourself from the school timetable, both for yourself and your kids are immeasurable. Here are just a few:

- Your kids will be well rested and less stressed, day in and day out.
- They can learn at a pace that suits them and not according to a one-size-fits-all framework.
- Homeschool groups and meet ups are mushrooming everywhere. These are good opportunities both for your kids to meet others doing the same thing but also for you to swap ideas and experiences with other parents. If there isn't one in your area, start your own. Your local library or community center might well provide a meeting room you can use for free and again, Yahoo Groups provides a good bulletin board for communicating about meet ups and events.
- You will not be locked into school holiday time schedules when it comes to traveling, thus saving money. Travel off-season and save major buckage!
- You will genuinely come to know your children, and they you, in a way that is just not able to happen when they spend most of their waking hours away from home. This is an opportunity for laying the groundwork for good communication with them that can last through their teenage years

and into adulthood.

Finally, a classic amongst homeschoolers across the board is David and Micki Colfax's early manifesto and raising four homeschooled boys who all went on to Harvard on full scholarships, Homeschooling for Excellence. OK, we are not all bound for Harvard, homeschooled or not, and there are many happy mediums in between. Also check out The New Global Student by Maya Frost. This family took their four teenage daughters out of high school against everyone's advice in order for them to spend several years traveling. The education they got as a result was beyond their expectations, and they all went on to competitive colleges at earlier ages than they would have done.

I homeschooled The Boy when we traveled around Europe for a year and for another full year when we moved back to England. While I won't lie that it had its challenges, it also gave us huge amounts of freedom for discovery and learning in non-conventional ways. I used a fully accredited homeschooling curriculum from Oak Meadow for most subjects and Aleks, which was originally developed by a team of cognitive scientists and software engineers at the University of California, Irvine, for math. I felt like any hardships of homeschooling were offset by the experiences he gained while traveling and, as an added bonus, he was not behind when he went back into conventional schooling when we returned home.

It is worth mentioning, a traveling single, homeschooling mom and her son far more intrepid than us and also among the most well known "World Schoolers" on the web, is Lainie Liberti and her son Miro who have been traveling around the world for years and blogging about it at Raising Miro.

There are loads of options when it comes to homeschooling and myriad ways of doing it in a way that works for your family – even as a single parent.

"We must, indeed, all hang together or, most assuredly, we shall all hang separately."
— Benjamin Franklin

#15 – CONSIDER CO-HABITATING

Housing costs are bar none our biggest expense as single parents and there is no reason to say that a purely traditional structure of a nuclear family, or single parent and kids, is the only option for how you live your lives. The trend for single parents to share living spaces is growing. Explore the organization Co-Abode for US-focused options.

While there are definitely pitfalls to these arrangements, with careful upfront planning and open communication, it can be done. The most successful ventures of this kind seem to be when both families set out parameters for managing different parenting styles, as well as expectations for the arrangement, at the outset.

Another rising trend is co-habitation with elders. Increasingly, housing programs are cropping up that create sharing options for young, old, and single alike. Homeshare, a mostly UK organization, pairs young or single people with elders usually in exchange for a small amount of rent and a set number of hours of care involving household help per week. In the United States, the National Shared Housing Resource Center again pairs homeowners with homesharers in exchange for an agreed level of support in the form of financial exchange, assistance with household tasks or both. For many seeking such arrangements, shared housing offers companionship, affordable housing, security, mutual support, while also preserving the fabric of neighborhoods, housing stock and providing alternatives to costly care homes for seniors. And if one of these seniors happen to be one of your parents, who is also well and able-bodied enough to help look after your kids when you're working or trying to keep your sanity, it can be a win-win situation in more ways than one.

"We are what we repeatedly do. Excellence, then, is not an act, but a habit."
— Aristotle

#16 – PRIORITIZE YOUR CREATIVE PURSUITS

Maybe you want to write a book, build a business, go back to school, knit a sweater, learn to Tango, but you wonder how you could possibly find time for any creative pursuits for yourself while keeping all the plates spinning in the air single handedly? There is an ancient Chinese proverb that is very apt here: Enough shovels of earth – a mountain. Enough pails of water – a river.

The point is you can do anything in baby steps. The continued action towards a goal, be it big or small, carried out on a regular basis over time, wins results. It is also good for you. Anytime or way you can give yourself a little extra space, will help you be a better parent in the long run.

There are two fantastic books published by 99U, a website dedicated to frontier ideas in culture, creativity, and entrepreneurship. Both of these books, Manage Your Day-to-Day and Maximize Your Potential, are a series of essays that are easy to dip in and out of and have great tips about creating productive habits and routines, no matter what your circumstances are or what you're ultimately working towards. Sometimes a few nuggets of wisdom, inspiration, or ideas to try make the difference between making the mountain seem scalable and you just wanting to pitch your tent at the bottom and not even try to climb it.

Not to mention the fact that it is important for kids to see parents involved in something we are passionate about. Through that they learn to respect that time we take for ourselves and ultimately find their own passions. This is also the best way to avoid the old living through your kids trap, so often exemplified by those sideline soccer or football dads, though the syndrome can manifest in many different forms. And finally, the more you are in tune and connected with the things that make you happy, the more you can see your child for who he is and not who you want him to be or hope he might become. At the end of the day, we all just want to be seen for who we are and the most important place for that to happen is at home.

"When you're used to being prepared to reject conventional wisdom, it leaves you open to learn more."
— Mayim Bialik

#17 – QUESTION ALL CONVENTIONAL WISDOM

This is a big one for me as I truly believe most people go through life without stopping to question such 'self-evident truths' as get-good-grades- so-you-can-go-to-college-so-you-can-get-a-good-job-so-you-can-get-a-mortgage-so-you-can-get-married, and so on.

While perhaps more myth than reality, the metaphor of lemmings going over the cliff following the masses is a powerful one. There is something liberating about getting to the point in life when you realize that you really needn't follow any else's rules for life other than your own. (OK, I'm not suggesting being a narcissist and breaking the law in any way!)

James Altucher, an entrepreneur who has both made millions and lost them again a couple times over, writes very useful little books that dissect such culturally, deeply held convictions about how life should be lived. Check out Choose Yourself and I Was Blind but Now I See! Also, Chris Guillebeau runs The Art of Non-Conformity blog and author of The $100 Startup among other books, which is a great resource for starting businesses on a shoestring, long-term travel while doing location independent work, and other such against the grain ideas.

Raising kids on your own, whether or not the other

parent is in the picture, is hard enough. Do not put yourself under even more pressure by trying to keep up with other people, be they family or friends' expectations as to how you should be governing your lives. If there is ever a time to flush the idea of "keeping up with the Jones" down the toilet, it is now.

"Piglet sidled up to Pooh from behind. "Pooh,"
he whispered.
"Yes, Piglet?"
"Nothing," said Piglet, taking Pooh's paw,"I
just wanted to be sure of you."
– A.A. Milne

#18 – MAKE TIME FOR FUN WITH YOUR KIDS

There will be times when you need to just chuck the schedules, the dishes, the chores, the play-dates aside, and go and spend time with just you and your kids. At the end of the day, that is all kids really want and need the most – your attention. And it's hard to give it to them in full measure when there are ninety-three other things to do in a day. So take time out, play hooky, or schedule an outing where you leave all distractions behind and simply go for a walk in the woods, a picnic, a trip to the zoo, or a museum, with just you and them.

I guarantee you will re-fill all of your reservoirs with time spent in each other's company, talking about life or estimating how many postage stamps it would take to encircle the world. You don't even have to go anywhere. Make Friday night pizza and movie night – making the pizza from scratch together.

Also, don't just come up with what you think would be a "constructive" or "educational" activity for you and your kids to do together. Meet him at his level and instead of trying for the umpteenth time to wrest the PS3 controller out of his hand, sit down and let him challenge you to a game of Battlefield 4. I have done this and I assure you I failed abysmally but we had fun and The Boy thoroughly enjoyed beating me and being far better at this than me.

I have found that parents of my generation waste far too much time, as I suppose our parents probably did too, bemoaning the nostalgia of the '70's and '80's and how grand life really was before cell phones, gaming, and the digital age. While newer does not always mean better, here's the news: kids growing up in the digital age need to learn how to navigate it and attempts by us to try to shoehorn them back to an analogue reality, is pointless and doesn't do anyone any favors in the long run. Embrace technology with your child and you can take the best that it has to offer, while helping him navigate his world. Done together, instead of continually fighting it, will make it more enjoyable for everyone along the way.

"Nothing you do for your children is ever wasted. They seem not to notice us, hovering, averting our eyes, and they seldom offer thanks, but what we do for them is never wasted."
— Garrison Keillor

#19 – LET THEM SEE YOU CRY

Look, you are not perfect so just stop trying to be right now. There are just going to be times where the façade crumbles and you kids are going to see you cry or yell like a bat out of hell. You are human and you have your limits and your kids might as well know that.

When this happens, if you can, call another single friend. Chances are ten to one they've been through it and even if they haven't, trust me, you're not alone. But when you've calmed down, go back to your kids and offer them an explanation, and if appropriate, an apology (especially in the case of losing control and yelling).

Perhaps conventional wisdom says you're the adult, why should you have to explain yourself or apologize for anything? But if you want your kids to respect you, you have to treat them with respect. And it never feels good to be yelled at and in the act of you acknowledging your actions and apologizing for behavior you might not be most proud of, they can learn a valuable lesson – to take responsibility for their own actions and that there is a standard by which we are expected to treat members of the family and loved ones.

You hold the bar higher for them, and for yourself, when you are willing to apologize when your behavior goes off course. And at the end of the day, we are all only human and never perfect.

"The whole is greater than the sum of its parts."
– Aristotle

#20 – A CHILDHOOD IS GREATER THAN THE SUM OF ITS PARTS

Sometimes single parenting can feel like an endless run with the torch to a never approaching finish line. It is inevitable to worry whether your approaches to managing all your lives and parenting is going to render your kid with years of therapy bills or if he might end up working at as a gas station attendant the rest of his life. This is normal. Do not fear. Chances are this is not going to happen and anyway, therapy is really very useful whether or not you hated your parents.

We all worry from time to time (or all the time) how much our kids will be damaged by the effects of divorce and whatever else happens in their childhood. But as we know, kids are resilient creatures, you survived and so will they. What doesn't kill us makes us stronger, as the saying goes. Truly, as long as you are there for your kids, they know they are loved by you unconditionally and can always count on you, they will be OK and you will make it through the rough spots. I once heard someone pass along a piece of wisdom, way before I ever became a parent, that has always stuck with me: Raising kids is easy, marinate them with love so by the time they are adults, they'll be ready for the world.

Truly, love expressed and time spent with your kids is more important than anything else you can give them. Among the many freelance jobs I juggle these days, one of them is outlining non-fiction books for authors before they write them. I recently worked with an author who is an expert in the field of youth and at-risk youth development. He wanted to call the book "Love is the Answer" but figured no one would take it seriously if he did. But all of his experiences working with kids all over the world have found that the single most important thing affecting kids' positive development is a relationship with a caring adult -- this could be a parent, teacher, coach, camp counselor, or other adult. And he has tons of research data to back this up. All I'm saying is, I'm not just making this love stuff up and I'll update this e-book with the information on his book once it's published.

"A pessimist sees the difficulty in every opportunity; an optimist sees the opportunity in every difficulty."
— Winston Churchill

#21 – BECOME AN UNBRIDLED OPTIMIST

It's no secret by now that optimism is good for your health. Researchers from the Mount Sinai School of Medicine have even found that looking on the bright side of things has long term, restorative effects and that resilient people weather life's hardships better than pessimists.

A long term study of Vietnam Veterans who were held captive in solitary confinement and tortured for six to eight years revealed several traits that seemed to set them apart in terms of their survival, and non-development of post-traumatic stress syndrome: optimism, altruism, a sense of humor, and having something to live for. All of these traits, are ones that we as single parents, surviving far less extreme circumstances I would venture to say, need to have in abundance – and by default, already do. There's a quote from The Life of Pi where the narrator has lost his entire family and is adrift on the open sea with a Bengal tiger for a traveling companion: "You might think I lost all hope at that point. I did. And as a result I perked up and felt much better."

Dr. Dennis Charney, the same leading expert and researcher on resilience who conducted the Vietnam Vet study, has also found that children, in particular, display remarkable resilience when faced with sources of stress in their environment. After years of research, he is a big believer in the fact that resilient kids, make resilient adults and writes "It has implications for how you might want to raise your children." He goes on to say:

If you grow up in a stress-free environment, you're not prepared for the inevitable stresses and strains that life presents. Everybody suffers the loss of loved ones. Everyone faces medical illness and meets with disappointment. The point is that you need to be prepared. I've done this with my own children. You need to take them out of their confidence zone. You give them challenges they can manage, and therefore learn from. And they develop a psychological toolbox they can call upon when faced with something difficult.

The main point here is that you have nothing to lose and everything to gain by making optimism your default setting. If you focus on the negative and hard aspects of your life, and "what might have been," that is then what you see. If you choose instead to focus on what you have, what you are grateful for, and believing that in most circumstances in life things have a way of working out for the best, you will not only be happier but you will create a happier, more positive environment for your kids to also not only survive in, but thrive.

Conclusion

I hope these 21 tips can serve as part of your personal toolbox for surviving the first few years of life as a single parent. Whether you're a single mom or dad, gay or straight, American or Icelandic, some of the issues you face might be slightly different, but many are fundamentally the same.

Keep these ideas in mind and before you know it, you'll be spinning more plates in the air than you ever thought possible.

If you have questions, comments, or suggestions on any of this, or even ideas of other topics you think I should include, please get in touch and share them through my website at www.hollyhudsonauthor.com.

Thanks for reading!

About the Author

Holly grew up in Ohio and a few other places around the world, which instilled in her a wanderlust she hasn't yet been able to outgrow. She's called Senegal, Tunisia, The Philippines, Mexico, Italy, Germany, Spain, England, and New York home at various points in her life. She graduated from Hampshire College in Massachusetts with a degree in film and theater.

These days, she lives between Ohio and London, England, or whatever other country might have her. She writes Young Adult and Contemporary Romance fiction and is the author of The Grace Steele Mystery Series and The Chemical Attraction Series, both available on Amazon. You can subscribe to her newsletter for updates on new releases by visiting www.hollyhudsonauthor.com

Made in the
USA
Monee, IL